ALLYSON COOPER

Cricut Maker For Beginners

All You Need To Know About Cricut Maker, Understand The Different Models And How They Work

Copyright © 2020 Allyson Cooper

All rights reserved

© Copyright 2020 - All rights reserved.

The content contained within this book may not be reproduced, duplicated or transmitted without direct written permission from the author or the publisher.

Under no circumstances will any blame or legal responsibility be held against the publisher, or author, for any damages, reparation, or monetary loss due to the information contained within this book. Either directly or indirectly.

Legal Notice:

This book is copyright protected. This book is only for personal use. You cannot amend, distribute, sell, use, quote or paraphrase any part, or the content within this book, without the consent of the author or publisher.

Disclaimer Notice:

Please note the information contained within this document is for educational and entertainment purposes only. All effort has been executed to present accurate, up to date, and reliable, complete information. No warranties of any kind are declared or implied. Readers acknowledge that the author is not engaging in the rendering of legal, financial, medical or professional advice. The content within this book has been derived from various sources. Please consult a licensed professional before attempting any techniques outlined in this book.

By reading this document, the reader agrees that under no circumstances is the author responsible for any losses, direct or indirect, which are incurred as a result of the use of information contained within this document, including, but not limited to, — errors, omissions, or inaccuracies.

CRICUT FOR BEGINNERS

Introduction 5

Chapter 1: What Is A Cricut Machine And How Does It Work? 14

Chapter 2: Cricut Explore Air 2 Vs. Cricut Maker 20

Chapter 3: Insights Of Explore Air 2 Machine 24

Chapter 4: Tools And Accessories Needed To Work With Explore Air 2 Machine 35

Chapter 5: Insights Of Cricut Maker Machine 40

Chapter 6: Tools And Accessories Needed To Work With Cricut Maker Machine 49

Chapter 7: How To Use Design Space 56

Chapter 8: Design Space Software Secrets And The Design Space App 65

Chapter 9: Best Projects You Can Do With Cricut Maker 75

Chapter 10: Best Projects You Can Do With Explore Air 2 86

Chapter 11: Tips And Tricks To Make Cricut Machines Easier And Efficient 96

Chapter 12: Best Software To Use With Cricut And Create Super Design Templates 102

Conclusion 109

Introduction

What is a Cricut Machine?

A Cricut machine is a cutting machine; it has the unique functionality of being able to cut different materials which you will need for your crafts and DIY projects. Some of these materials include paper, vinyl, and materials as thick as wood. Although they are hardware, Cricut machines are dependent on their connection with your devices like mobile phones and computers.

Cricut machines are a very fun tool to make use of because they allow you to create art from materials you may not have known existed, and they allow your creativity to take flight. With the use of Cricut machines, you are able to create new materials to aid your work, and these materials you create may not be found otherwise.

In a nutshell, you create designs and templates using the device to which your machine is connected (the phone or computer system). These designs are preloaded into the device which your Cricut is connected to, and you can make a lot of changes or modifications with these designs. These designs are what you pre-load into the Cricut and make use of them to cut/print the material you are looking to use, just the way you want it to be.

When it comes to how a Cricut works, there are a lot to be learned about it, but having access to your own Cricut machine is like opening yourself up to a whole new world. There is literally no limit to the number of awesome crafts you can make with the use of the Cricut machine.

How the Cricut Works?

Considering the kind of magic the Cricut performs, you may be tempted to ask how it is able to achieve all these. Before you really begin to ask these types of questions, let us take you on a tour of the answer.

The Cricut works by printing out already-defined designs on a piece of material that will be fed into the machine. What this means is that if you are going to make use of a Cricut to create a design on any material, you have to go through these processes to make the most out of your experience.

Popular Cricut Machine Models - Which is the Best to Go For?

These models all have their characteristics, which make them advantageous over the next and a few setbacks that would make you want to go for the next one above the other one. In this portion, we will take a closer look at these and this will help guide you into the exact Cricut you can get for yourself the next time you are looking to make a purchase of the machine.

Cricut Explore One

The Cricut Explore One is a fun and relatively easy-to-use tool that is most suited for a range of DIY hobbies. This machine is meant for everyday-home applications to cut regular materials and is not really built to take on heavy materials or to be used at an industrial scale. This model of the Cricut machine is easy to be mastered following the ton of guidelines that can be found with it or even over the internet. It can cut through materials of up to 12 inches width and is meant for cutting, scoring, and writing on materials.

The Cricut Explore One comes without the double tool holder feature, is relatively slow with the execution of tasks (when compared against other more recent Cricut models), and has a limited amount of power it can accept to pass through it beyond which it will get faulty. It can be connected to the device that will be used for programming the design onto the machine using a host of options, including the USB functionality, and wirelessly using the Bluetooth feature.

If you are new to the world of Cricut designing and you are looking for a quick tool that comes with the basic functionalities of cutting, printing, and writing, which you can wrap your head around almost immediately, and it is relatively cheaper (especially if you are strapped for cash), then you may want to go for this option. For use, this model of the Cricut is compatible with the free iOS, Android, Windows, and Mac operating systems, and this implies that you can basically make use of it across a number of devices, including your phones and PCs.

This is what this model of the Cricut looks like:

Cricut Explore Air 2

This model of the machine comes with a few more functionalities than the one discussed above. For one, it can cut through a host of materials that the other one mentioned earlier cannot cut through, and it comes with many more perks since it appears to be an improvement of the former model.

The Cricut Explore Air 2 is an equipment that allows its user to create more designs and permit his creative genius to surface even more than if he were using the former one. This is because this model of the machine comes with the ability to flawlessly and perfectly cut through at least 100 different material types, including those that are not easily cut through, like vinyl, iron-on, and the likes of these.

In addition to just cutting materials, this model allows the user to personalize his projects by branding them with designs that he so chooses to, it also helps him to create home-made gifts and even custom-design apparel. Built to last, this machine comes with the special ability of durability. It has the ability to withstand a lot of wear and tear, and this is justifiable since it has to be subjected to a lot of pressure every time it has to cut through a material. Despite all the nuances of this machine, one of its most redeemable qualities is that it is easy to learn. Because of the vast array of materials this Cricut can cut through, it is most suited for a wide range of DIY hobbies; it can cut through materials of up to 12 inches in width. This model of the Cricut is faster than the Cricut Explore One and has the print and cut capability, which makes working with it even more fun than it ordinarily should be.

As it is the case with the Cricut Explore One, this model is also compatible with the free design application that is obtainable on the iOS, Windows, Android, and Mac platforms. Connecting the machine to your internet-enabled device can be achieved using wireless connections like Bluetooth, and also the USB connection feature that is available.

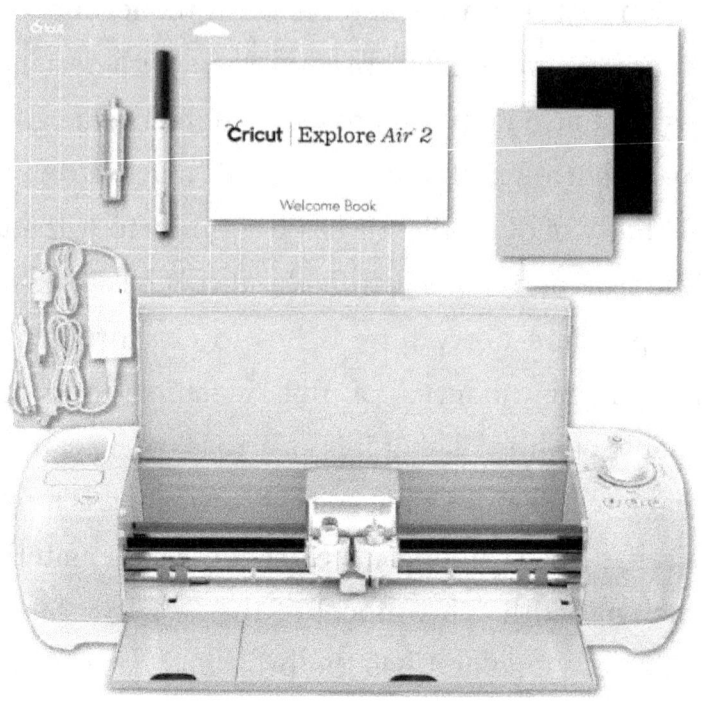

Cricut Maker

This is another model of the Cricut machine. This model is considered to be among the top-ranking Cricut machines and is used for more demanding and professional DIY tasks and performances. Suited to take on materials of up to 12 inches in width, the Cricut Maker can cut up to 300 and above materials, which include the more-difficult-to-cut materials like wood. The Cricut Maker has a high durability level and, considering the usability of this machine, it is easy to be learned following the guide that the Cricut machines come with, or with explainer content scattered across the internet.

The Cricut Maker has a wide range of adaptability as it can be used for a host of tasks, including cutting, writing, scoring, and other professional effects that need a more detailed machine that possesses extra features. This model of the machines comes with a double tool holder and possesses the ability to perform tasks at a rate that is faster when compared to other Cricut machines that have been discussed earlier; up to 2 times as fast. The Cricut Maker supports the print and cut feature, which allows the user to get more creative with the tasks at hand, and opens up the doors to a wider range of craft opportunities. The Cricut Maker is 10 times more powerful than other Cricut machines and so can make a lot of designs and DIY crafts.

Just like the others, it is operated by connecting it to the design space application that is free and available on the iOS, Android, Windows, and Mac platforms. The connection between the machine and the powering device can be established wirelessly using the Bluetooth connection, or by making use of the USB cord as provided alongside the machine.

Cricut Joy

It is the last model of the Cricut machine we will be discussing. First off, this is a little machine that permits you to cut, draw, and make designs out of numerous materials, counting vinyl, cardstock, paper, and a few more materials. One of the redeeming qualities of this machine is its size, which makes it easy to be transported and easy to use as well.

As opposed to other Cricut machines, this particular model seems to be able to hold up its own forte, although the small size will usually make people tend to roll their eyes and dismiss it as being the last option to choose when faced with options. This, however, is not the case of the Cricut Joy as it possesses some features that make it a great choice, especially for those that uphold the practice and lifestyle of minimalism. Here are a few of them;

- This machine can create cards in record time. This is as a result of the CardMat feature that it comes with.
- With a weight of approximately 3.9lbs and dimensions (in the sealed box) of about 8.4x5.4x4.2 inches, it is amazing that this machine can cut up to 50 different materials and makes very precise cuts because of the built-in cutting technology.
- Even without the Cricut Mat, which is an integral part of the other Cricut machines, this machine is able to make

very precise cuts. This machine supports the continuous cut feature, which allows the user to make cuts that are up to 20ft long.

- This machine comes with access to the free design space app that is available across all platforms and software operating systems. Connectivity is usually established using a wireless component like the Bluetooth connection.

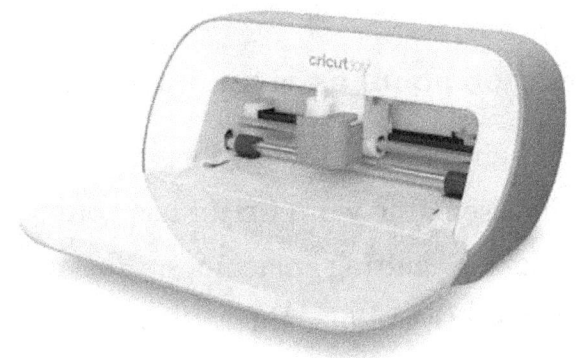

-

Chapter 1: What Is A Cricut Machine And How Does It Work?

Basic Information about a Cricut Machine

While the brand envelops a few distinct items, including heat presses and embossers, the word Cricut has gotten synonymous with kick-the-bucket cutting machines. So, in case you're wondering, what is a Cricut machine? The appropriate response is a home pass on cutting machines utilized for papermaking and different expressions and specialties.

Basically, it's a savvy cutting machine known as the "flawless passage point to the universe of exactness making."

It's imperative to realize that these machines are not just utilized for cutting paper. They're made to cut a wide assortment of material in astonishing manners. Vinyl is another material that is related to kick-the-bucket cutting machines, just as felt, cardstock, thus numerous others. They can even cut wood!

Notwithstanding cutting a wide range of materials, the machines that are presently accessible can likewise draw with pens, compose with pens, and score material for fresh, easy collapsing.

Setting Up Step by Step

Opening the Box

When you purchase a bundle from Cricut, you will receive a few boxes, but the most significant box amongst them will hold the Cricut Maker. To recognize it, you'll see the picture of the Maker on the box.

When opening the Cricut box, the first thing you see is the welcome package placed on the machine. This contains a welcome manuscript, a rotary blade with cover, a fine point pen, a USB cable, and a packet with your first project.

When you take the Cricut machine out of the box, the power cord will be underneath along with the cutting mats. You will also see half of the settings on the dial between the fabrics. This is for when you need a little less or a little more force than is given by the programmed settings. If you cut a light cardstock, for example, but the knife doesn't completely cut the design, you can pick the half setting between Light and Cardstock. Or if you cut a poster board and the blade exerts too much pressure by slicing your pad, simply select the arrangement between the cloth and the poster board. If you use another product and face it, you can use this tool well over a hundred different materials, so why wouldn't you? All you need to do is just to change the dial to the setting "Custom". You can then pick the exact product you are using from the massive drop-down list in Design Space. And again, the Cricut changes its blade settings automatically so that you don't have to.

Unwrapping

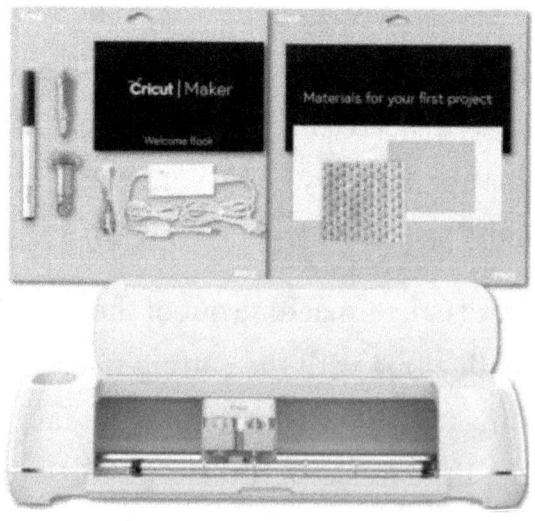

The Cricut machine is wrapped with a layer of cellophane and a protective wrapper. Before setting up the device, you have to remove the wrappings.

Some Styrofoam protects the in-housing of the machine, and that has to go too.

Your Cricut Maker will also come with some supplies; you should unwrap them and check them out. Lucky for you, the fine point blade is already installed in the Cricut Maker, so you don't have to bother with that.

Visit Cricut /setup

The following step in setting up your machine lies in the technical aspects. Cricut has a webpage dedicated to walking you through this process, which makes it super easy.

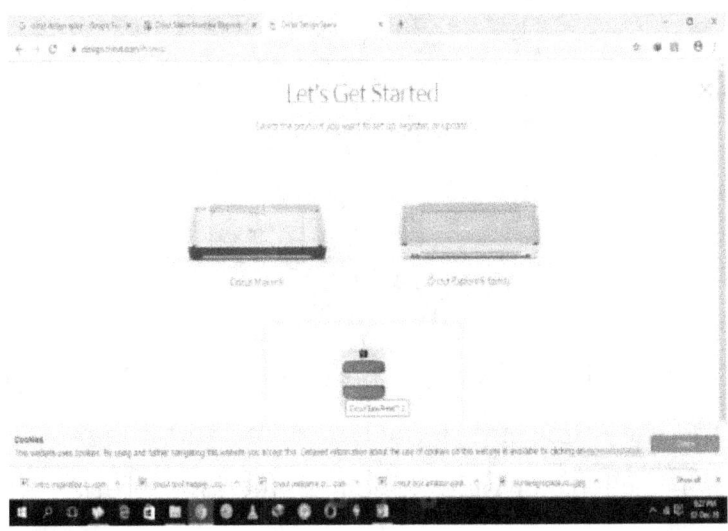

Open Cricut /setup on your device. You can use any device that is compatible with Cricut like a smartphone, tablet, or computer. When you do that, you will be asked to install Cricut Design Space and also sign up. Then, you'll be given your Cricut ID.

If you have been using a former Cricut machine before, then you can carry on with your former ID.

Plugging It In

Then, you need to take your USB cord and the power cord to power up your Cricut machine.

This will be shown on the setup wizard of the webpage.

For the USB cord, you connect the square end to the Cricut Maker device and the other end to the computer and, the power cord is easy to connect from Cricut Maker to the power outlet.

Claim Your Bonus

After plugging in your Cricut, you will be able to claim a free welcome bonus from Cricut, which is a free month of Cricut Access. This means that you get to enjoy access to projects, fonts, and Cricut Cut Files.

Begin Your Project

If you need a little something to practice with before starting on your intended project, Cricut Maker machines usually come with a little project in the welcome pack to help you get acquainted with the tools.

The Maker comes with all the tools that you need to complete the project, which is usually the task of making a little card.

After this, you can begin using it. The thing is, when you want to use your Cricut Maker, you need to learn how to use Cricut Design Space.

Chapter 2: Cricut Explore Air 2 Vs. Cricut Maker

Cricut Maker

- They have a faster cutting ability.
- They write at a much faster rate compared to other Cricut machines
- They are made up of the rotary blade, which is used for fabric.
- They can cut many more materials than the other Cricut machines available.

Cricut Explore Air 2

- They also get to cut more materials.
- They are made up of fast mode, which aids them in cutting fast.
- The writing speed is also fast.
- They are made up of two holders used for keeping tools.

Cricut Explore Air

- Just like the Air 2, they also contain two holders for holding tools.

- They are Bluetooth enabled.
- They are made up of a dual carriage used for wiring and cutting.

Cricut Explore One

- They are a very useful electronic cutting machine for DIY crafts and projects.
- They are handy for the cutting of different materials ranging from paper and iron-on to adhesive vinyl as well as leathers.

The Cricut maker is the latest Cricut machine and is the very best of all the Cricut machines available, although this might vary according to the purpose of the user. It has about ten times cutting force compared to Air 2, which shows that it has the highest cutting capacity.

The Difference between the Cricut Maker and Cricut Explore Air 2

The following features are those of the Cricut maker that distinguishes it from the Explore Air 2:

- It is made up of the Rotary blade, which is mostly used for cutting fabrics. It is also used in cutting leather, silk, and other materials.
- In the Maker, the scoring pen is replaced by the scoring wheel, which has more delicate scored lines and sharper.

- The Maker is made up of the knife blade used for thick and heavy materials such as balsa wood and heavy chipboard.
- It can use the Digital sewing pattern library, which provides access to hundreds of fabric plans for an instant cut.
- It can cut hundreds of materials ranging from the finest paper to heavy fabrics.
- Unlike the Explore Air 2, the Maker comes without the dial.
- The Maker is also made up of a ridge that is used for placing your tablet devices as well as redesigned storage areas.

Cricut Explore Air 2

- In terms of cost, the Cricut Explore Air 2 offers the best value for money. It has lots of great features despite costing up to half of the price of the Maker.
- It can be used for a variety of projects such as the patterned vinyl t-shirt, reverse canvas project, vinyl on glass water bottles, craft cutting, etc.

The Difference between the Explore Air 2 and the Explore Air

- Both the Explore Air 2, as well as the Maker, can cut, score, and write twice faster than the Explore Air can.

- Unlike the Explore Air that comes in the blue color, the Explore Air 2 does come in pastel colors.

Irrespective of their differences, they are similar in some areas:

- Air and Air 2 are both made up of a dual carriage that allows cutting and writing without having to change any tools.
- Another notable similarity between these machines is that they both work with the deep cut blades and fine point.

Chapter 3: Insights Of Explore Air 2 Machine

The Cricut Explore Air 2 is the latest model in the Cricut Explore family. It is the mid-range machine and is the best one for anyone starting out with crafting and cutting machines.

It comes in a few different colors such as rose, mint, blue, and black. It is a versatile machine that is easy to pack away and store, but big enough to do large designs with. It comes with a few different cutting blades, which give the user a lot of cutting material choices.

The Cricut Explore Air 2 is a fast, accurate machine that makes precision cuts. It comes with dual accessory housing. The housing houses both a drawing pen or a scoring pen and a blade, without having to swap out accessories during a cut.

The Cricut Explore Air 2 Features:

- DIY hobbyists, beginners to crafting, scrapbookers, and gift card designers.
- The machine is capable of writing, scoring, and cutting.
- The Explore Air 2 is easy to set up.
- It is easy to use.

- The machine has a Smart Dial for manual selection at the machine level for certain materials.
- The Smart Dial can also be used to set up the material cutting depth selection.
- Both the material and depth selection can also be set up within Design Space, the design software available to Cricut users.
- The weight and dimensions of the Cricut Explore Air 2 are:
    - Weight = 16 lbs.
    - Dimensions = 24" x 9.5" x 9.5"
- It comes in the following colors:
    - Rose
    - Blue
    - Black
    - Mint
- Bluetooth connectivity comes standard with the machine.
- The machine has USB connectivity.
- The Cricut Explore Air 2 is compatible with over 100 different types of materials.
- It does NOT work with the Card Mat or any of the Smart Materials.
- The maximum material width of the Cricut Explore Air 2 is 12 inches.
- The commercial-grade cutting technology available for the Cricut Maker is NOT available for the Explore Air 2.

- Design Space is the design software of choice for Cricut machines and comes free with each device.

What Comes in the Box?

The following items come packed in the box of a new Cricut Explore Air 2:

- The Cricut Explore Air 2, in the color it was purchased in
- A welcome booklet for the Cricut Explore Air 2
- A power cable for the machine
- A USB cable for the machine
- 1 Cardstock material sample to practice with
- 1 Cricut Premium Fine-Point blade
- 1 Cricut Premium Fine-Point blade housing
- 1 Cricut 12" x 12" StandardGrip machine mat (green)
- 1 Black Cricut Fine-Point Pen

Added extras that come with the Cricut Explore Air 2 are:

- Cricut Access 30-day trial membership
- Access to free Cricut Design Space sewing patterns
- Access to free Cricut Design Space projects

Setting Up the Cricut Explore Air 2

Setting up the Cricut Explore Air 2 is a quick and easy process.

- Unbox the Cricut Explore Air 2.

- Find a place to set the machine up. Ensure there is enough space, at least 10 inches behind and in front of the machine.
- The surface you use must be flat and non-slip.
- Make sure there is a power source close by to connect the machine to.
- There must be enough space for your connected device (PC, Laptop, etc.) as well.
- Take off any packaging tape or protective coverings on the device.

Connecting the Cricut Explore Air 2

First Steps to Connect the Cricut Explore Air 2:

- Once you have your Cricut Explore Air 2 positioned, you can plug the power cable into the round port at the back of the cutting machine.
- Plug the other end of the power cable into the wall socket.
- Place the small, square side of the USB cable that came with the machine in the port to the left of the power socket on the back of the cutting machine.
- Place the other end of the USB cable into the device you will be using with the Cricut Explore Air 2 to run Design Space.
- On the PC, laptop, or mobile device you're using, open your web browser.

- Go to the Cricut setup page
- Switch on the Cricut Explore Air 2 by pressing the "Power" button on the machine, located at the top of the Smart Dial.
- Open the machine by pressing the "Open" button located on the left-hand side of the machine.
- If you are a first-time user on the Cricut Design Space site, you will need to fill out the form to create a user ID.
- Once you have created the user ID, you will be prompted to "Get Design Space plugin". Download the plugin by following the easy and concise on-screen instructions.

Connecting a Device to the Cricut Explore Air 2 Using Bluetooth:

- You must first follow the above steps to connect the machine and create a user ID.
- Go to the Bluetooth settings on the device you want to attach to the Cricut.
- Select the Cricut Explore Air 2 device from the available Bluetooth devices.
- It will ask you for a code. Type in 0000 to pair the Cricut Explore Air 2 with your device.
- The "Power" button on the Cricut Explore Air 2 will turn blue when it is connected to a Bluetooth device.
- If you have created your Cricut user, open the browser on your Bluetooth device.
- Go to the Cricut Design Space website

- When you go to download Design Space, it automatically detects the operating system of the device from which you logged into the software.

Your login details, unless you opt not to have them do so, will be remembered from your last login on Design Space.

Setting Up the Cricut Explore Air 2 and Installing Design Space on a PC

All the Design Space downloads below will require an internet connection for laptops and desktops running Windows or Mac operating systems.

Using Design Space on a Mac

These instructions are for desktop and laptop devices running the Mac operating system.

The minimum requirements to install Design Space on a Mac device are:

- Mac OS 10.12 or later versions are compatible with Design Space.
- The device must support either USB or Bluetooth.
- 1.83 GHz is the minimum CPU requirement.
- 4GB is the minimum RAM requirement.
- 2GB is the minimum amount of free hard drive space required.

- 1024px x 768px is the minimum screen resolution required.

Downloading and Installing Design Space for Windows:

- Open the internet browser on your device to the web page
- Select "Download".
- The download will begin and will indicate its progress. This can take a few minutes, depending on the speed of your internet connection.
- In the "Downloads" folder on your Mac, you will find the following dmg file:
- Cricut Design Space Install v5.11.57.dmg (the version number may differ depending on the updated version.)
- You will need to drag the Cricut Design Space Install v5.11.57.dmg file into the "Applications" folder.
- Double-click on the Cricut Design Space Install v5.11.57.dmg to launch the application.
- If at any time the operating system on your device prompts you to download the application from the internet, click "Open." Otherwise, Design Space will not install.
- It is a good idea to create a desktop icon for the Cricut application to make it easier to find. To create a desktop icon, drag the Cricut Design Space Install v5.11.57.dmg into the "Dock" folder.
- You will need to "Sign in with your Cricut ID" once the installation is finished.

Using Design Space on Windows

These instructions are for desktop and laptop devices running a Windows operating system.

The minimum requirements to install Design Space on a Windows device are:

- Microsoft Windows version 8 or later versions are compatible with Design Space.
- The device must support either USB or Bluetooth.
- 1.83 GHz is the minimum CPU requirement.
- 4GB is the minimum RAM requirement.
- 2GB is the minimum amount of free hard drive space required.
- 1024px x 768px is the minimum screen resolution required.

Downloading and Installing Design Space for Windows:

- Open the internet browser on your device to the following web page
- Select "Download".
- The download will begin and will indicate its progress. This can take a few minutes, depending on the speed of your internet connection.
- In the "Downloads" folder on the PC, you will find the following file:

Cricut Design Space Install v5.11.57.exe (the version number may differ depending on the updated version.)

- If at any time the operating system on your device prompts you about trusting the application, you must select to trust the application. If you do not trust the application, it will not install.
- You must follow all the on-screen install prompts.
- It is a good idea to create a desktop icon for the Cricut application to make it easier to find. It usually automatically creates a desktop icon. If not, the application can be found in the "All Programs" taskbar.
- You will need to "Sign in with your Cricut ID" once the installation is finished.

Setting Up the Cricut Explore Air 2 and Installing Design Space on a Mobile Device

You will need an internet connection or data to download Design Space on a mobile device.

Using Design Space on Android

These instructions are for mobile phones and tablet devices running an Android operating system.

The minimum requirements to install Design Space on an Android device are:

- Android 6.0 or later versions are compatible with Design Space.
- Most of the later versions of Android mobile phone devices are compatible with Design Space.
- Most of the later versions of Android tablet devices are compatible with Design Space.
- It should be noted that Chrome books are not compatible with Design Space.

Downloading and Installing Design Space for Android:

- Go to the Google Play Store on your Android device.
- Search for the Cricut Design Space app.
- Install the app on your Android device.
- You can either set up the machine right away or skip over the machine setup step to go to the design section.

Using Design Space on iOS

These instructions are for mobile phones and tablet devices running an iOS operating system.

The minimum requirements to install Design Space on an iOS device are:

- iOS 11 or later versions are compatible with Design Space.
- iPhone 5s and later models are compatible with Design Space.

- iPad Air and later models are compatible with Design Space.
- iPad, iPad mini 2, and later models are compatible with Design Space.

Downloading and Installing Design Space for iOS:

- Go to the App Store on your iOS compatible device.
- Search for the Cricut Design Space app.
- Install the Cricut Design Space app as you would any other iOS app.
- You can either set up the machine right away or skip over the machine setup step to go to the design section.

Chapter 4: Tools And Accessories Needed To Work With Explore Air 2 Machine

Cricut has different models of die-cutting machines and for a beginner; you may be confused about the type that is best for you in the course of crafting. Look no further as I have you covered. I have four machines (Cricut Maker, Cricut Explore Air 2, Cricut Explore Air, and Cricut Explore One) to give insight into their strength and weaknesses while making up your mind to which one of them you will work with.

The type of Cricut machine you may wish to get depends on the type of the project you want to use it for. All Cricut machines have certain things in common including cut, right, and score, a 12" wide cutting area size, can cut a variety of materials, use Design Space software, and "Print Then Cut" feature. What stands them out are the differences between them as will be discussed:

- Double /Single Tool Holder: the main tool holder is what you see when you open the lid of the Cricut machine, designed to move back and forth on the carriage. Double tool holder allows you to write and cut in one step while the single tool holder will do the same function in separate steps. Among the four mentioned Cricut machines, only Cricut Explore One has a single tool holder while the rest has a double tool holder.
- Adaptive Tool System: this is a recent addition to the Cricut machine and available only to Cricut Maker. The adaptive tool system delivers more power to the cutting force (4 kg) which is ten times more than the nearest versions to it; uses a steering system to control the direction of the blade, adjust the pressure of the blade automatically with each cut pass, and uses a new set of tools and accessories for diverse cuts.
- Fast Cutting Mode: this mode is used to write and cut materials twice as fast, especially when producing large quantities of materials. This feature is common to Cricut Maker and Explore Air 2.
- Cutting with Bluetooth: this feature is common to the Cricut Maker, Explore Air 2, and Explore Air. You can use it to cut your material without using a cable.
- All models of Cricut machines have a slot for cartridge and can be linked to your Design Space account to have access to your cartridge graphics. Newer models like the Cricut

Maker come with a digital Design Space library instead of the physical cartridge and if you need to connect a physical cartridge with it, you will need to buy a separate cartridge adapter.

- Tips on How to Use the Cricut Explore Air Effectively
- Test the material you wish to cut first before starting the real project. This will ensure the smooth delivery of the project without encountering any problem. Look out for materials such as fabric, wood, or felt because they can pose all sorts of trouble during the cutting process.
- Roll the Cricut mat backwards away from the material you have finished cutting instead of peeling the material away from the Cricut mat. This will give you a project cut with precision.
- Always clean your Cricut mat after you finish a project. Use a lint roller over the Cricut mat to remove leftovers of dirt and lint from the surface of the mat.
- Organize your blades and knives separately. This will help you apply the correct blade or knife for a particular project. Mixing them up may cause you to use an inappropriate blade for a project which might lead to damage or blunting the blade.

Best Tools and Software for Cricut Explore Air Machine

- Extra mat: make sure that you have an extra mat handy while doing your project. It could be difficult while doing your project if you discover that your Cricut mat is no longer sticky or messing up your work.

- Weeder tool: this tool is particularly useful when lifting vinyl material. There are varieties of weeder tools including Cricut Weeder Tool, Weeder Toolset, Dental Picks, and Pin Pen, and Exacto Knife. They all do the same function and I encourage you to experiment with all to discover which one works for you.
- Tweezers: this tool is a weeding tool that can help you lift materials on the mat, especially vinyl from the middle and not necessarily from the edge. It can also be used to pick up tiny little scraps from the surface of the mat.
- Scrapper Tool: this tool is used to get bubbles out of vinyl materials on the mat. This will help you to get clean cuts and ensure that your materials are not distorted while cutting the fine details.
- Brightpad: this tool is useful for tracing and adapting patterns to your material. It also makes the cut lines visible.
- Trimmers/Cutters: when you need to cut your material in a straight line, then this tool comes in handy especially when the need to size your material on the mat arises.
- Spatula: This tool is useful when lifting a material that can be torn easily from the Cricut mat. This tool is also used to clean the mat from dirt and debris.

- Scissors: this tool is well-known for cutting fine details in small areas when the need arises.
- Brayer: this tool is useful for stabilizing materials before you begin the cutting process. It helps the material to stick to the Cricut mat without damage.
- Cricut EasyPress: this tool is essential for heat transfer of vinyl materials. It saves you a lot of peels after one or two wears.
- 'Sure, Cuts A Lot' is third-party software that allows you to cut any shape you can imagine with ease. It is easy to use with many electronic cutting machines including Cricut Explore/Maker machine, CraftRobo/Graphtec, Vinyl Express, and more. To work with your Cricut Explore machine, use 'Sure Cuts A Lot' to design your shape then export it to your Cricut machine Design Space using a compatible file format. It is a wonderful software for craftsmen. Give it a try, you will not regret it.

Note that this software requires a firmware update to your Cricut Explore machine; includes freestyle drawing tools, uses auto trace features, and with more than 200 shapes built-in.

Chapter 5: Insights Of Cricut Maker Machine

Cricut Explore Air 2 is an equipment that helps a lot in some or all stages of creative work such as Sewing, Scrapbook, Party Scrap, Home Decor, Stamping, Custom Stationery, Making Stickers, Making EVA pieces and also helps who works with Painting because with it you can make stencil your way, very personalized.

In this manual, we'll not only stay on theories, but we will teach how to use Cricut Explore Air 2! That's right! So, let's get your hands dirty, installing your machine so you can make the first cut, as well as showing you some creative techniques that can be done with it!

How to Install Cricut Explore Air 2

First step: Take your Cricut Explore Air 2 out of the box and check out all its components:

- Power cable
- USB cable
- 01 Premium Blade and Thin Tip Blade Holder already pre-installed

- 01 Standard cutting base (StandardGrip) or Light Fixation (LightGrip) 30.5 cm x 30.5 cm (12 in x 12 in)
- Welcome Book
- Materials for the first project
- 01 Fine tip pen in black color
- The software provides you with 50 ready-to-use projects

Items checked successfully; now it's time to choose where your machine will be.

Here's a tip: to use it, remember to place it in space enough to leave 25cm in front and 25cm behind.

So now press the "OPEN" button...

Wow!

Like magic, an automatic opening is present in front of you! You can take the bucket because you drooled too much!

Now with great care, remove the seals and protections from all the parts you find.

Now, to get to know a little more about your Cricut Explore Air 2, notice that it has an Intelligent Panel on the right side, which already contains the cutting settings for the most used materials in everyday life. However, it cuts out more than 100 materials, but we will talk about that later.

In the central part, there are two "drawers" to store blades and tools. Also, on the left side, there is a compartment for tools and pens. Finally, there is an entrance to connect physical cartridges that are still used by people who bought files in this mode in older versions of Cricut machines.

Now that they are appropriately presented let's start by installing the Design Space, following the steps below.

How to Install Cricut Design Space

Access Design Space in your browser.

Select the Product you want to Configure/Register. Here, we'll go with Cricut Explore Product Family" option.

Design Space is available for Android and iOS, in addition to Windows and iMac. For cellular systems, there is an offline version of the program. However, on the computer, the offline version is still beta, so it is not available to all users.

TIP:

If your screen is in other languages, remember that you can download and install the Google Translate extension on your computer, this way almost the entire process will be in English.

The next screen prompts you to log in with your Cricut account. If you don't already have a Cricut ID, create it on this screen. However, if you already have a Cricut ID, click on the "Login" button and enter your login and password.

After logging in, click on "Download".

Wait for the download to complete.

When the download is complete, the Cricut icon will appear in the file name.

Click on the ".exe" file to install.

Finally, follow the instructions on the screen.

Click "Finish". However, it is important to know that your machine is automatically registered during its configuration.

Click "Continue".

How to Connect Your Cricut Explore Air 2 Machine

It's time to plug in your Explore Air 2 and turn it on.

If you prefer, you can also connect it via Bluetooth, since it is already integrated with Cricut Explore Air 2.

However, if you need help pairing your computer to Cricut Explore Air 2 via Bluetooth, you'll get to see a more detailed explanation before the end of this portion. It can be done at any time so that we can proceed with the connection via USB cable.

With the machine turned on, the installation process itself checks whether the firmware is up to date or not.

After verification, the next screen shows you the option to subscribe to Cricut Access or not. This is the Cricut store, where you can find thousands of image files, projects, fonts, and many beautiful creations.

You can have a free month to try and then cancel your subscription at any time, or you can choose to subscribe later. However, if you decide not to sign at this time, don't worry! There are many free designs available for you to use.

Well, going back to the subject, the next screen is where it all starts, and you can follow step by step all the commands in detail. Therefore, use the materials and tools that come with the machine: papers, Cricut black pen, and the blade.

Above all, you must follow each step of the guidance and add a little more so that you begin to understand the process of creating a piece. Pretty cool. Practical and gradual learning!

Well then, let's proceed to learn about the accessories and the creative possibilities of your Cricut Explore Air 2.

Cutting Base, Cutting Blades and Accessories

Now let's talk a little bit about cutting bases, blades, and other accessories that you can use on your Cricut Explore Air 2, in addition to showing some creative possibilities.

- Cutting bases

There are four types of cutting bases, and all of them can be used in Cricut Explore Air 2. Therefore, for purging, each floor has a color to differentiate the glue's adhesion from each one.

They are:

- Blue base = light fixation
- Green base = standard fixation
- Pink base = specific for fabrics
- Purple base = for heavier materials.

Important:

The Purple Base is not required for use with Cricut Explore Air 2 because it is more targeted at materials of greater thickness that are cut in the Cricut Maker, but if you want to use it, no problem.

- Cricut Cutting Blades

With four types to choose from, the blades that can be used on the Cricut Explore Air 2 are:

For materials up to 1.1mm:

- Fine Point Blade (silver) is ideal for cutting materials such as paper, thinner acetate, vinyl, transfer, tracing paper, and other materials.
- Premium blade (slightly golden) - has more extended durability than the traditional Ponta Fina.
- Fabric Blade (light pink) - for thinner fabrics. It is the same as the Ponta Fina blade, but the holder's color is

different so that you can identify each one's function. In this way, you preserve the cutting edge and help to prolong the durability of your blades.

- Deep Cut Blade - For materials up to 1.7mm, it cuts EVA, thin cork, among other thicker materials precisely.

Changing the blades is very simple and cost-effective, even better because once you have the support, you only need to purchase the tip, that is, the blade, in fact!

Other tools and accessories will also give your pieces a special touch.

You know that perfect continuous crease, beautiful to live in?

Well, the Crease pen is responsible for all of these. Therefore, its role is essential to make folds in boxes, invitations, or even give an extraordinary detail to part of the project. It supports "A" on the cart's left side while the blade supports "B."

These pens can also be great allies to your creativity. Like the crease pen, Cricut pens are used in the "A" support of the cart.

Cricut has several types: Fine point, medium point, with sublimation ink, and even washable pen for fabrics. Yes! You draw, sew your piece, wash it, and the paint comes out, and the finish of your work is perfect!

Cut with EVA?

Yes! The Deep Cutting Blade makes it easy to work with more material options. There are lots of these practical and straightforward bookmarks, but you can create much more!

Working with Stamping

T-shirts, stuffed animals, bags, caps, shoes, backpacks, and whatever else your imagination sends! Cricut has so many types of heat transfers that we don't even know where to start! The desire is to use them all at once!

Another type of printing material that Cricut supplies are Infusible Ink. The materials in this line have sublimation technology that you can wash without worrying about whether it will come out or fade after washing.

Therefore, when using Infusible Ink materials, you can make 100% polyester fabrics and many other materials that come with stunning and vibrant colors!

Here we only put a little bit of what your Cricut Explore Air 2 is capable of!

There is a lot more!

So, let's work that Cricut Explore Air 2 is waiting for you to make incredible creations!

Below you learn how to configure the Cricut Explore Air 2 to use via Bluetooth.

How to Use Cricut Explore Via Bluetooth

However, remember that this form of connection is optional but very useful for those who do not have much space to leave many wires on the table or bench where they work. Therefore, you can even work with the device away from Cricut, considering a maximum distance between 3m to 4.5m.

First, to use Bluetooth, your computer must also have this device. Most of them already come with Bluetooth.

To check if your computer already has Bluetooth, right-click on the "Start" button and click on the "Device Manager" option.

Therefore, if Bluetooth is listed among the options, it means that your computer already has it.

However, if Bluetooth does not appear on the list and you want to use it, you can buy a Bluetooth Dongle device to allow the configuration of your computer with other equipment via Bluetooth.

Remember: if you don't have Bluetooth installed on your computer, that doesn't stop you from using your Cricut Explore Air 2. Just connect it via USB cable and be happy!!

Now that we know if your computer has Bluetooth or not close the Device Manager.

If your computer already has Bluetooth installed, it's time to set it up!

Chapter 6: Tools And Accessories Needed To Work With Cricut Maker Machine

Right now, there are five unique edges and various accessories to either score or draw with your Cricut. Look at an outline of the entirety of the tools you can use with any of the Cricut family machines.

Cricut Maker and the entirety of the tools inside it:

Fine Point Blade

The fine point cutting blade is the most well-known sharp edge, and it accompanies the entirety of the Cricut Machines. It is made of the German Carbide, which is an incredibly solid and great material most ordinarily utilized for cutting tools materials.

This sharp edge is ideal for making mind-boggling cuts, and it's intended to cut medium-weight materials. It used to be silver; however, it presently arrives in a lovely brilliant shading.

Profound Point Blade

In the event that you have to cut thicker materials, the Deep Point Blade will be your closest companion. You can utilize it with any of the Cricut Explore Family machines or potentially Cricut Maker! The edge of this cutting blade is such a lot more extreme— 60° contrasted with 45° for the fine point sharp edge—This truly permits the edge to infiltrate and cut mind-boggling cuts in thick materials.

Reinforced Fabric Blade

The Bonded Fabric Blade was explicitly intended to cut texture. Try not to utilize this sharp edge for some other sort of material. You will demolish your cutting edge! There's a major admonition with this cutting edge, however. The texture you are going to cut should be clung to a sponsorship material. In the event that you are a sewer, you may comprehend what reinforced texture; yet on the off chance that resembles me and have no related knowledge with textures, let me disclose to you genuine speedy.

Cutting Edges, Black Pen and Scoring Stylus

Fundamentally, the support is a kind of material—like heat and security—that you have to follow—security—to your textures so as to be cut with this sharp edge. Consequently, the name of Bonded Fabric Blade.

Scoring Stylus

The Scoring Stylus is a tool that permits you to make an overlap on your materials. It's ideal for making boxes and card making.

Cricut Pens

The Cricut Pens are stunning, in light of the fact that you can cut and score. However, you can likewise compose on your materials. The Pens permit you to make a progressively customized project.

Print Then Cut

This isn't simply a tool; however, it is an element that permits you to print—on white shading paper—your plans and afterward cut them. This is extraordinary if you are into organizer stickers, designs, card making, and so on.

The Cricut Maker bolsters everything! Look at all of the subtleties, so you can see the capability of this machine. The Cricut Maker permits you to utilize the entirety of the accessible tools and highlights of the Explore, and this is the reason I get increasingly slanted to prescribe the Maker. I know it's increasingly costly; however, you find a workable pace with your machine since gossip has it that there are more tools coming up soon.

Note: The Print Then Cut alternative permits you to print on hued paper!

Blade, Scoring Wheel and Rotary Blade

- Rotating Blade

The Rotary Blade cuts through, essentially, any kind of texture. What's more, the best part is that you needn't bother with any sponsorship material to balance out the texture on the tangle. That by itself ought to get you too cheerful!

This sharp edge likewise accompanies the Cricut Maker (this is a serious deal since you regularly need to purchase these sorts of tools independently or in a pack) and must be utilized with the "Fabric Grip Mat".

- Blade

This cutting edge is the thing that makes the Cricut Maker an absolute making machine. The blade edge is the most grounded of all, and with it, you can cut extremely solid materials, for example, thick calfskin, balsa, and basswood.

The projects you can do with this child are simply stunning. You can make wood signs for your home, boxes, amazingly strong cake toppers, and that's just the beginning.

Fast Swap Tools

Not at all like the remainder of the cutting edges that have an alternate lodging, The Quick-Swap framework permits you to utilize five unique tools (2 sharp edges, and 3 hints).

- Perforation Blade
- Scoring Tip
- Wavy Blade
- Engraving Tip
- Debossing Tip

Something cool, and that I am very appreciative of, is that you can utilize these tools with a similar lodging and that, my companion, rises to reserve funds! We should see, somewhat progressively, pretty much these tools.

The Scoring Wheel is a device that permits you to make lovely, tense, and firm overlap on your resources. To supply you with the finest outcomes, Cricut has structured this tool with two distinct tips, 01 and 02. Contingent upon the resources you hand-picked, Design Space will propose to you the tip that's required.

The Engraving Tip is something that numerous crafters have been hanging tight for! With this tool, you'll have the option to etch a wide assortment of materials.

The Debossing Tip will shove the resource in, and it will make wonderful and point by point structures. The debossing will carry your projects to an unheard-of level due to the detail you would now be able to add to your structures.

With the Wavy Blade as opposed to cutting on straight lines like the turning or fine point edge, this tool will make wavy impacts on your polished products.

The Perforation Blade permits you to do projects with a tear finish. With this tool, another universe of conceivable outcomes has open. You can make coupons, wager tickets, and so forth!

Weight and Color:

The Cricut Explore Air 2 comes in such huge numbers of hues, yet the maker just accompanies three which are Champagne, Blue, and green.

Extra room:

The two machines have great stockpiling for the tools and edges that they are equipped for utilizing. The Maker has much more stockpiling than the Explore. I like this since I am ready to store more treats in it.

Cartridge Slot: B

Before, you could purchase physical Cartridges and associate them with your machine. A Cartridge has a lot of pictures or potentially prepared-to-cut projects; presently, these Cartridges can be purchased inside the product itself, with that goal, that's the reason the Maker doesn't have space for them.

Smart Set Dial:

It permits you to choose from a scope of supplies earlier when you cut. I LOVE this since it has the most well-known materials for you to look over. A few people like to choose them on the product. I PREFER the dial.

Adaptive Tool System:

This framework is the thing that makes the Maker 10X more grounded than any of the Explore Family Machines. This innovation controls the heading and of the cutting edge steadily. Reality be said, this tool is astounding to such an amount that it can change the pressure of the sharp edge to coordinate the materials you are working with!

Docking Station:

The Maker permits you to dock your telephone or iPad over the machine. On the off chance that you plan on utilizing your iPad or Phone, this is a cool component. There's additionally a USB port that permits you to charge your gadget also.

Chapter 7: How To Use Design Space

Purchasing a Cricut is futile if you don't learn exactly how to master Style Room since you will always require this software to cut any kind of job. In my opinion, Cricut Style Room is an exceptional device for newbies, and also if you have no experience with any other Layout programs like Photoshop or Illustrator, you will certainly discover that, although it looks overwhelming, it's quite simple.

Layout Space, it's mainly to touch up your projects and create marginal designs with Forms and Fonts.

If you desire something a lot more innovative, you are most likely to need your own designs or Cricut Accessibility. There's a subscription where you obtain access to their supergiant library. Find out more about it in this write-up and also the guide I create.

When you log into your Cricut Design Area account and also intend to start or modify a new project, you will certainly do every little thing from a window called canvas. The Canvas Location in Cricut Style Space is where you do all of your modifications prior to you cut your tasks.

There are numerous switches, options, and points to do that you might feel shed. Do not worry, I am below along the way, applauding you up and motivating you to keep going. In this publication, you are about to learn what each and every single symbol on the Canvas area is for. To keep every little thing in order as well as easy to understand, we are going to divide the canvas into 4 areas and also 4 colors:

- Top Panel Yellow-- Modifying Area
- Left Panel Blue-- Insert Location
- Right Panel Purple-- Layers Panel
- Canvas Location Green

Pointer: This is not a short message, so I encourage you to get a cup of coffee with some donuts or cookies if possible.

Top Panel Cricut Design Space

The top panel in the Style Space Canvas area is for editing, enhancing, and preparing aspects on the canvas area. From this panel, you can pick what type of font style you'd like to use; you can transform dimensions, straighten styles, as well as other features! This panel is divided into two sub-panels. The very first one permits you to save, name, and finally reduce your jobs. And also, the second one will enable you to regulate and also modify points on the canvas area.

Sub-panel # 1 Name Your Project and Cut it

This sub-panel enables you to navigate from the Canvas to your account, projects, as well as it additionally sends your completed projects to cut.

Toggle Menu

When you click on this button, one more entire menu will move openly. This menu is a useful one. However, it's not part of the Canvas, and that's why I won't be entering into a lot of detail. Primarily, from here you can most likely enter your profile and also transform your photo.

There are various other useful and technological points you can do from this Menu like calibrating your maker, blades; additionally, updating the Firmware-- Software-- of your tool. You can as well manage your memberships from Cricut Accessibility, your account details, and more. I suggest you to click on every web link to make sure that you discover every little thing that Cricut Style Room has for you.

Note: On the settings 'choice', you can transform the visibility as well as measurements of the Canvas; this is explained much better at the end of this article when I describe everything about the canvas area.

My Projects

When you click "My Projects", you will certainly be rerouted to your collection of points you have currently developed; this is excellent because often you may wish to re-cut a previously developed job. So, there's no need for you to recreate the same job over and over.

Save

This option will certainly turn on after you've placed one component on your canvas area. I suggest you save your project as you go. Although the software program is on the cloud, if your browser accidents, there goes your hard work with it!

Maker-Explore (Machine).

Depending upon the sort of maker you have, you will certainly require selecting either the Cricut Maker or the Cricut Explore Machine; this is really crucial because on the Cricut Manufacturer you will discover choices that are only readily available to that specific maker. So, if you have a Maker and you are making with the Explore alternative ON you won't be able to turn on the tools that are for the maker.

Make It.

When you are done posting your files, and also ready to cut click on "Make it"! Your tasks are separated by mats according to the colors of your task. From this home window, you can likewise boost the variety of projects to cut; this is excellent if you are planning on developing greater than one cut.

Subpanel # 2-- Modifying Food selections.

It's incredibly useful, and also it will certainly help you to modify, prepare, and also organize font styles as well as pictures on the Canvas Location.

Undo & Redo.

Occasionally while we work, we make blunders. These little buttons are a great means to correct them. Click Undo when you develop something you do not want such as or make a mistake. Click Redo when you inadvertently remove something you didn't wish to erase or modify. (If only there was something comparable forever itself lol).

Line Type and Fill

This option will inform your equipment what tools, as well as blades you are going to utilize. Bear in mind that relying on the Maker you have actually picked on the top of the home window (Manufacturer or Discover), you will have different choices.

Line type

This alternative will inform your device when you are cutting your job, what device you will certainly be using. Right here and now, here are seven choices (Draw, Cut, Engrave, Wave, Deboss, and Perf). If you take a Cricut Maker, all choices will certainly be readily available, however, if you own an Explore you will solitarily have the Cut, Draw, and the Score choice.

Right at this point is a much more comprehensive description of a piece tool.

Cut

Lest you published a JPEG, otherwise PNG photo to the Canvas. 'Cut' is the defaulting line type that every one of your basics on your canvas will certainly have; this means that when you press 'make it', your maker will certainly cut those designs.

With the Cut choice chosen, you can transform the fill of your components. At the end of the day, this converts in the different shades of materials you will certainly utilize when you cut your jobs.

Draw

If you intend to create on your layouts, you can do it with your Cricut! When you appoint this line type, you will certainly be prompted to choose any one of the Cricut Pens you have (You require detailed pens, unless you have a 3rd event adapter). When you select a specific layout, the layers on your canvas area will certainly be outlined with the shade of the pen you picked. With this tool, when you click on "Make it"; rather than reducing, your Cricut will certainly create or draw. Keep in mind: This option doesn't tint your styles.

Score

Score is an extra powerful version of the Rating line situated on the left panel. When you appoint this attribute to a layer, every one of the designs will certainly show up scored or rushed. This time, when you click on 'make it', your Cricut won't cut, yet it will score your products. However, keep in mind the wheel just collaborates with the Cricut Manufacturer.

Engrave, Deboss, Wave, as well as Perf

These are the newest tools that Cricut has released for the Cricut Maker, and with them, you will have the ability to create incredible results on various sorts of products. I do not have these tools yet due to the fact that they will certainly be coming out in a number of weeks, once I have them on my hands, I will certainly offer you a quick upgrade.

Fill

The fill option is primarily to be used for printing as well as patterns. It will only be triggered when you have cut as a "line type." Do not fill in forms that will not print anything. Print is by far, one of the best functions Cricut has due to the fact that it enables you to print your styles and then cut them; this is remarkable, and truthfully, it's what motivated me to obtain a Cricut in the first place. When this Load alternative is active, after you click "Make it"; first, you'll send your data to your home printer and afterwards, have your Cricut do all the hefty training.

(Cutting) One more excellent choice for the Print Kind is Patterns!!! You individuals, this is so trendy. Usage Cricut's options, or publish your own; you can include a pattern to practically any kind of layer. Let's claim it's Valentine's Day. You can make a stunning card with a currently developed pattern from Cricut Access (Subscription, not totally free), or your own. After all, it prints as well as cut at the same time.

Select All.

When you need to relocate all of your components inside the canvas area, you may have a hard time to select them individually. Click "Select all" to pick all of the elements from the canvas.

Edit

The cut and also copy option will certainly be turned on when you have a choice of several elements from the canvas area. The Paste choice will certainly be made it possible when you duplicate or cut something.

Align

If you have experience with various other visuals style programs, more than likely you'll recognize just how to utilize this food selection. If you aren't aware of the Align Equipment, let me tell you something; the Align Food selection is something that you intend to understand perfection.

Here's what every align feature means:

- Align: This function permits you to align all of your layouts, and also, it's turned on when picking two or more elements.
- Line up Left: When utilizing this setting, all of the aspects will certainly be lined up to the left. The furthest aspect to the left will certainly determine where all of the various other components will certainly move towards.
- Align Right: When using this setting, all of your components will certainly be straightened to the right. The outermost aspect to the right will certainly dictate where all of the various other elements will certainly relocate.

Chapter 8: Design Space Software Secrets And The Design Space App

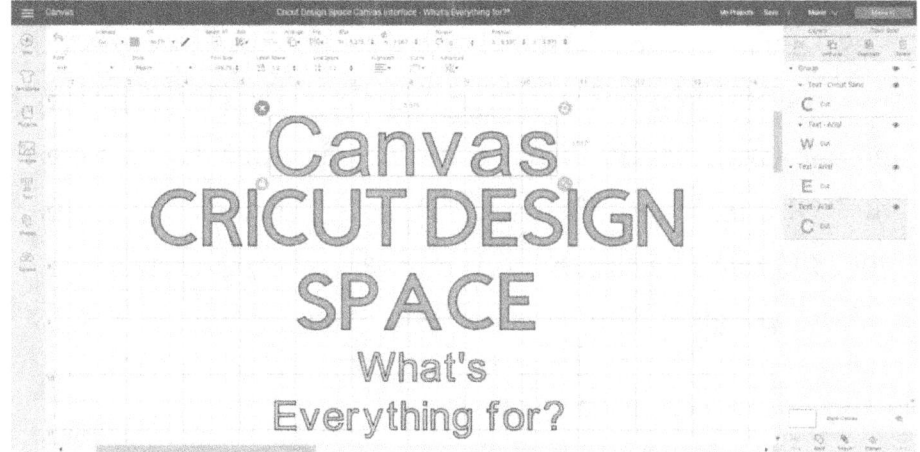

What Is Cricut Design Space?

Cricut Design Space is a software created by Cricut which permits smooth communication with your machine by telling it what to do.

With the software called Cricut Design Space, you can upload your own images and fonts in various file formats (JPG, PNG, SVG, etc.) and control them to match your various designs.

As of January 2020, the design program can only be accessed through the desktop app version. When I downloaded my app, I just clicked the link and was directed to download it. I then followed the on-screen guides to install it on my PC, but you can as well install it through your Mac.

Features of Cricut Design Space

The following are various Design Space features that are available across Design Space platforms: Attach, Bluetooth Connection, Contour, Cut & Write in one Step, Flatten to Print, Writing Style Fonts, Machine Setup, Print then Cut, Slice, and Weld, System Fonts, Offline, Photo Canvas, 3D layer Visualization, Smart Guide, Snapmat, Pattern Fills, Templates, Image Upload, Link to Physical Cartridges, Curve Text, Knife Blade Cutting.

Using Cricut Design Space

Cricut Design Space is an amazing tool in making your <projects idea; at the beginning, the learning may seem very difficult but never you worry as time goes on you will get over them soon. When I started using the Design Space, everything looks new to me not until I sat down last summer; gave more time, patients, and concentration and finally I figured it out. You too can achieve it, if you are really determined to.

About some weeks ago I went to a friend's house only to see a brand-new machine based on my recommendation, but guess what, the challenge he had was how to use the Design Space. All

I did was to take him through the basics, as soon as I was done, he was very grateful I came. Right now, he can use the Design Space all by himself. One of the ways of successfully going through the Design Space is to start from the known to the unknown by understanding how things work when you make simple use of predesigned projects.

As we go through the step-by-step guide on using the Design Space, bear in mind that you will start simply by selecting a design that is already created for you in Cricut Design Space.

1. Open your Cricut Design Space on your computer but, as for me, I like using the app.
2. Click on the square showing "Create New Project". You will be taken to the design area where the whole miracle is done.
3. Click on the image of your choice at the bottom of the screen.
4. Click on the square at the top and type in what you would want to make. If what you needed to do is to appreciate those who attended your wedding last weekend. Just type in, "Appreciation Card". You can think of other words and find out for yourself.
5. After you have selected your project, click the "Insert" button at the bottom of the screen.
6. Now your project is in the workspace. Click on the arrow pointing to the right and scroll through to see each mat

that you will be using. I always like looking through them and get my paper ready in the manner they will be cut.

7. Then scroll back to the beginning and click on the "Continue" green circle. The Design Space will guide you through, so just follow the instructions as they pop up. Whenever you are working in the design space it will ask you to connect with a nearby device. Don't worry, this is actually okay.

8. The project I chose during my Appreciation Card design uses the scoring stylus. I think you would love that because it will be so helpful.

9. Ensure the style is all in the way. You must click as soon as it is down. Then shut the latch and it's all complete.

10. The flash keys on the machine are next to the press. The essence of the initial one is aimed at loading, while the second starts scoring and cutting. As soon as you are at it, be sure the dial is set on the material you are using.

11. The prompts will continue to pop up following the steps. This will tell you when and how to load and unload.

I enjoy seeing the Machine cut my design. It is so amazing for me every moment. In making my Card, it all took me about half an hour and I had Cards and envelopes ready to send gratitude to all my wedding guests. Now is over to you. You can achieve this! If I did, all you need to do is to start with something simple so you can get used to the design space and its workability.

Tips and Tricks to Make Projects

- Starting New Project:

Generally, there are 2 ways to start a new project which are: from the design tab or from the project tab.

Tip: Ensure your project is saved as you continue working to enable been saved up in the cloud for later use during cutting and design. As soon as your project is saved, it can easily be accessed through a desktop computer, laptop, iPad, or phone.

Let's go all the way to starting a new project from the Design tab.

Step I: You will open the Cricut Design Space app to the Design tab.

Step II: You have to sign in to your Cricut ID by tapping the Account menu. To show that you have successfully signed in, the Account menu sign will showcase a checkmark in it.

Step III: Click on the "New Project" button.

Now let's look at starting a new project from the Project tab.

Step I: You will open the Cricut Design Space app to the Projects tab.

Step II: You have to sign in to your Cricut ID by tapping the Account menu. As soon as you have successfully signed in, the Account menu icon will showcase a checkmark in it.

Step III: You have to tap the project tile labeled "Start a new project from scratch".

- Saving A Project:

Tips: As you continue with your project Design, ensure you save it to be available in "My Projects" on your Desktop computer, iPad, or any other device you are using for future use. Starting a new project on your iPad or PC will prompt you to save or discard it. As soon as you click discard, you will never see it again in your system. However, ongoing projects on your iPad are saved automatically in your iPad. Even if you decide to leave the app suddenly and later return back to it again, it will remain the way you left it. But bear in mind that it is not saved to the cloud unless you push the save button.

Step I: You will open the Cricut Design Space app on the Design tab.

Step II: Tapping the Account menu will prompt you to sign in using your Cricut ID.

Step III: Immediately you are signed in, the Account menu icon will appear with a checkmark in it.

Step IV: Then save the project, the menu should be tapped while you select "to save."

Step V: In the case of the project tab, the saved project will display as a project tile in the project tab.

- Accessing Saved Project:

Tips: You can access your projects via your Mac, PC, or iPad using the Cricut Design Space app. As soon as you tap outside the project preview pane, it will dismiss and you will be returned back to "My Projects". You can bypass the project preview pane by double-tapping on a project tile directly in the Design tab.

Step I: You will open the Cricut Design Space app on the Project tab.

Step II: You will sign in to your Cricut ID by tapping the Account menu.

Step III: Immediately you are signed in, the Account men icon will appear with a checkmark.

Step IV: You will have to select "My Projects", by tapping the Project menu.

Step V: Projects that are saved using the Cricut Design Space app will show you a preview image in the project tile. If you want to continue, tap the project tile.

Step VI: The project preview pane is like this:

Customize: It opens on the design screen for you to make changes to the project.

Date Modified: If there were any Modifications done previously it will display here.

Delete: Once this choice is selected, your project will be completely deleted from the list of Projects saved.

Duplicate: This option enables you to duplicate your project. Meanwhile, your duplicate project will be assigned a fresh name.

Make It Now: opens the project director in the mat preview, to enable you to make your project without any alterations.

Preview: It displays the project as positioned on the design screen.

Price: Discounts on the project price is made based on your images price or your subscription.

Project Name: This has to do with the particular name you wish to give your project.

Project Resources: This represents your larger images in the project on a small scale. If you want to view it on a larger scale, scroll down.

Step VII: Close to the Picture, you will see images that are required to complete your project. Below each image is a display of whether you own it, the image available on subscription, free image, or the price of each.

- Sharing Your Projects:

The very essence of Design Space is to derive inspiration so you can inspire others too, that is why any project I make I love sharing it with the Cricut Community. Below are the steps I took in sharing my Projects.

Tip: Sharing of Project is possible now on Windows/Mac and iOS platforms but not yet ready on Android.

Step I: Sharing a project on Pinterest or Facebook, you have to open a design Cricut website in your browser, preferably Chrome.

Step II: Insert your Cricut ID and password, and then sign in.

Step III: If the login is successful, click on the "View All" link at the top of the 'My Projects' toolbar.

Step IV: Go through your list of already made projects and choose the one you would love to share with the Cricut Community.

Step V: You can now click on the share link at the down part of the tile. Design Space will ask you to add more information.

Step VI: By clicking on Add Details, your project will open in edit mode.

Step VII: For uploading a photo of your project, you should click on the addition button below the photo's header. You will select a photo from your desktop.

Step VIII: In case you wish to turn your image, use the rotate control.

Step IX: You will use the Zoom control to size your image up to a limit of 300% larger than the normal size. You will use your mouse to do navigation.

Step X: Ensure the project toggle is visible to others by moving the toggle to the right.

Step XI: To edit your project name, just change the title of your project so that other users of Cricut will be able to comprehend.

Chapter 9: Best Projects You Can Do With Cricut Maker

Vinyl Decals and Stickers

One of the projects you can carry out with the Cricut Maker is the cutting of vinyl and stickers.

You just have to create your design in Cricut Design Space, instruct the Maker to cut, then weed and transfer the design to whatever surface you choose.

Fabric Cuts

The presence of the Rotary Blade in the Cricut Maker makes it a well-respected machine. The Maker can cut any type of fabric including; chiffon, denim, silk, and even heavy canvas. With this machine, you can definitely cut huge amounts of fabrics without using any backup, and this is because it comes equipped with a fabric cutting mat. Awesome machine!

Sewing Patterns

One major benefit of owning the Cricut Maker machine is the extensive library of sewing patterns that you'll have access to.

The library has hundreds of patterns, including some from Riley Blake Designs and Simplicity; all you need to do is select the pattern you want and the machine will do the cutting.

Balsa Wood Cuts

The Knife Blade coupled with the 4kg force of the machine means that the Cricut Maker can easily cut through thick materials (up to 2.4mm thick).

With these features, thick materials that were off-limits for earlier Cricut Machines are now being done.

Thick Leather Cuts

Just like Balsa wood, the Cricut Maker is also used for thick leather cuts.

Homemade Cards

Paper crafters use the Cricut Maker because the power and precision of the machine make the cutting of cards and paper far quicker and easier. With the machine, homemade cards just got better.

Jigsaw Puzzles

With the Cricut Maker, crafters can make jigsaw puzzles because the Knife Blade cuts through much thicker materials than ever before.

Christmas Tree Ornaments

Cricut machine owners can easily make Christmas tree ornaments. All you have to do is to go through the sewing library for Christmas patterns, use any fabric of your choice to cut out the pattern, and sew them together. Remember the Rotary blade cuts through all sorts of fabric.

Quilts

Thanks to the partnership between Cricut and Riley Blake Designs, Cricut Design Space now has a number of quilting patterns in the sewing pattern gallery.

The Cricut Maker is now used to cut quilting pieces with high precision before they are sewn together.

Felt Dolls and Soft Toys

The "felt doll and clothes" pattern is one of the simplest designs in the sewing pattern library. Thus, it is used for homemade dolls and toys.

The process is easy; just select the pattern you want, cut, and then sew.

T-Shirt Transfers

The Cricut Maker is used for cutting out heat transfer vinyl for crafters to transfer their designs to fabric. To achieve this, you have to make your design in Design Space, load the machine with your heat transfer vinyl, cut the material, and then iron the transfer onto the t-shirt. Alternatively, you can use the Cricut EasyPress to transfer the vinyl.

Baby Clothes

The Cricut Maker cannot cut adult clothing patterns because the mat size is only 12'x24. However, you can easily make baby clothing patterns with the machine.

Doll Clothes

Just like baby clothes, the Cricut Maker can easily make doll clothing patterns because the mat size is big enough.

Fabric Appliques

The bonded fabric blade doesn't come with the Cricut Maker, but if you buy it, you will be able to use your machine to cut complex fabric designs like appliqué. For the bonded fabric blade to cut effectively, there has to be bonded backing on the material.

Calligraphy Signs

The stand out feature of the Cricut Maker is the Adaptive Tool System. With this feature, the machine will remain relevant in the foreseeable future because it fits with all the blades and tools of the explore series, as well as all future blades and tools made by Cricut.

The Calligraphy pen is one of such tools, and it is ideal for signing and card making.

Jewelry Making

For crafters that like to explore jewelry making, the power of the Cricut Maker means that you can cut thicker materials, and while you can't cut things like diamond, silver or gold, you can definitely try to make a beautiful pair of leather earrings.

Wedding Invitations and Save the Dates

Weddings are capital intensive and we all know how the so-called 'little' expenses like STDs and invitation can add up to the huge cost. However, if you have the Cricut Maker machine, then you can make your invitation and STDs yourself.

The Maker is capable of making invitations of the highest quality. It cuts out intricate paper designs and the calligraphy pen is very useful too.

Wedding Menus, Place Cards, and Favor Tags

The Cricut Maker is not restricted to the production of pre-wedding Invitations and STDs. With the machine, you can also produce other items such as place cards, wedding menus, favor tags, etc.

In order to keep the theme front and center, the crafter is advised to use a similar design for all their stationery.

Coloring Book

With the Cricut Maker, you can make 'mindful coloring' books from scratch. To achieve this goal, you need a card, paper, and a beautiful design. Then you command the Cricut Maker to create your personal and completely unique coloring book with the aid of the Fine-Point Pen tool.

Coasters

In the sewing library, there are a number of beautiful coaster patterns and as such, the Maker is used to coasters.

With the Cricut Machine, you can work with materials such as metallic sheets, quit, leather and everything in between.

Fabric Keyrings

The Cricut Maker makes fabric keyrings and the process is simple – It cuts out the pattern and then sews it together. Besides, there are a number of designs for fabric keyrings in the sewing pattern library.

Headbands and Hair Decorations

The Cricut Maker is known to cut through materials like thick leather and this has gone on to inspire the production of intricate headbands and hair decorations. The machine is so inspiring; crafters in the fashion world use it for creative designs and projects.

Cut-Out Christmas Tree

It is a normal tradition for people to buy Christmas trees during the holiday season. However, if you don't have enough space for a big tree in your living room, or maybe you're allergic to pine, then you can definitely create your own Christmas tree.

The production of an interlocking wooden tree is something the Cricut Maker does easily because the blade is capable of cutting through thick materials like wood. With the Cricut Maker, you don't need a laser.

Cake Toppers

When Cricut bought over the Cake cutter machine, the idea was to create shapes made of gum paste, fondant, and others.

It is obvious that the Cricut Maker can't cut as good as the Cake machine; however, it can be used to produce tiny and intricate paper designs that can be used to decorate cakes.

Fridge Magnets

Cricut machines like the Maker and Explore air are capable of cutting out magnetic materials. Thus, crafters can use the Maker to make those fancy magnetic designs placed on refrigerators.

Window Decals

If you're one of those that love to display inspiring quotes on your window or even fancy little patterns on your car, then the Maker got you covered. You just have to load the Maker with window cling and get your design created.

Scrapbooking Embellishments

The Cricut Maker is used for embellishments when scrapbooking. It is public knowledge that Cricut machines are super when it comes to cutting intricate designs. However, the Cricut Maker takes it to a whole new level, and the responsive new blades take away all forms of complexity.

Craft Foam Cuts

In the past, Cricut machines found it difficult to cut craft foam (especially the Explore Machines), however, the Cricut Maker, with the 4kg of force cuts through craft foam very easily.

Boxes and 3D Shapes

The Cricut Machines comes with a Scoring Stylus and this tool can create items with the sharpest edges imaginable.

We all know that the Cricut Maker can execute all kinds of sewing patterns thrown at it. It can also cut paper crafts including 3D shapes and boxes.

Stencils

The Maker comes in handy for people that create things that are used to create other items. The machine is incredible for making stencils, bearing in mind that you can utilize thicker materials to create the stencils.

Temporary Tattoos

If you're one of those people that want to have tattoos, but don't want them permanent for life, then the Cricut Maker is your go-to machine.

With the Cricut Maker, you can etch your design on tattoo paper (mostly coated with transfer film) and use it on your skin.

Washi Tape

Crafters that use Washi tape for scrapbooking can testify to how expensive it can be, especially when buying in bulk from craft stores. However, those that own the Cricut Machine can use it to cut out Washi sheets – they can print and cut their personal designs on it.

Addressed Envelopes

The Cricut Maker is an astounding machine that can save you from spending on certain items. Remember we talked about making handmade wedding invitations; with the Cricut Machine, you can also make envelopes to go with the cards. Another good feature about the machine is that it is equipped with a Calligraphy pen and a Fine-point pen, meaning that it is capable of addressing your envelopes automatically. All you need to do is to make sure that the words are clear enough for the postman to read.

Glassware Decals

With a Cricut Maker, you can cut vinyl to make glassware designs. People that host themed parties will love this one; e.g. if you're hosting a summer house party and you're serving mojitos, then you can decorate your drinking glasses with coconuts and palm tree decals. Also, people holding Xmas parties can design and cut themed stickers to use on their cups.

Decorations

There are a couple of other desktop craft machines that are used to create general household decorations, but the Cricut Maker is one of the best – If not the very best.

With the Cricut Maker, you'll be empowered to create 3D wall hangings, beautiful cut-outs in the living room and even things like signage in your closets, etc.

Cushion Transfers

With your Cricut Maker, you can brighten up your cushion and pillows by adding your homemade designs. With the flocked iron-on vinyl, you can create a lovely textured cushion by using heat transfer vinyl on the Cricut Machine.

3D Bouquet

The machine takes us back to the wedding theme once more.

Remember, with intuitive tools like the scoring stylus and the Fine-Point, the Cricut Maker is superbly equipped to carry out intricate papercrafts. Thus, you can introduce a touch of homemade crafts to your wedding, or even create flowers to design your home, knowing that you don't have to water them.

With the Cricut Maker, you can have yourself a lovely, beautiful and immortal bouquet.

Chapter 10: Best Projects You Can Do With Explore Air 2

Cutting Letters and Shapes for Scrapbooking

Shapes are one of the most vital features in Cricut Design Space. They are used for creating some of the best designs. In this tutorial, you will learn how to cut letters or texts, how to add shapes and how to adjust the size, colors and rotate shapes.

To add a shape;

1. Log into your Design Space.
2. From the drop-down menu, click "Canvas". You will be taken to the canvas or work area.
3. Click "Shapes" on the left panel of the canvas.
4. A window will pop-up with all the shapes available in Cricut Design Space.
5. Click to add shape.

We have explained the process of adding a shape. Now, to cut a shape;

1. Click "Line type". Line type lets your machine know whether you plan on cutting, drawing or scoring a shape.
2. Select "Cut" as Line type and proceed with cutting the shape.

Cutting Letters

1. First of all, you need to add the text you want to cut. Click "Add Text" on the left panel of the canvas.
2. Place text in the area where you want to cut it. Highlight the text and click on the slice tool. If you have multiple lines of texts, weld them and create a single layer. Then, use the slice tool.
3. Move the sliced letters from the circle and delete the ones you don't need.

How to Make Simple Handmade Cards

If you want to test your crafting skills, the Cricut Explore Air 2 has made it possible for you to be creative with designing whatever you want to create on the Design Space. We will be teaching you how to use your Cricut Explore Air 2 to make simple cards.

1. Log into Design Space with your details. Do this on your Mac/Windows PC.
2. On the left-hand side of the screen, select "Shapes". Add the square shape.
3. By default, there is no rectangular shape, so you have to make do with the square shape. However, you can adjust

the length and width. You can change the shape by clicking on the padlock icon at the bottom left of the screen. Change the size and click on the padlock icon to relock it.

4. Click "Score Line" and align.
5. Create your first line. It's advisable you make it long. Use the "zoom in" option for better seeing if you are having difficulties with sight.
6. Select the first line you have created and duplicate. It's easier that way than creating another long line. You will see the duplicate option when you right-click on your first line.
7. Follow the same duplication process and create a third line.
8. Rotate the third line to the bottom so that it connects the other two parallel lines you earlier created. Remember to zoom in to actually confirm the lines are touching.
9. Duplicate another line, just like you did the other. Rotate it to the top so that it touches the two vertical parallel lines. You should have created a big rectangular shape.
10. Highlight your rectangular shape (card). Select "Group" at the upper right corner.
11. Now, change the "Score" option "cut". You can do this by clicking on the little pen icon.
12. Your lines will change from dotted to thick straight lines.

13. Select the "Attach" option at the bottom right-hand side of the screen. The four lines will be attached and will get the card ready to be cut on the mat correctly.
14. You can adjust the size of the card as you like. At this point, you can add images or texts; beautify your card anyhow you want it.
15. After you are done, select the "Make it" button and then "Continue" to cut your card out.

If you don't know how to create a style on your cards with shapes, follow these simple steps to create one.

1. Select your choice of shape. Let's choose stars for example. Select the "Shape" option and click on the star.
2. Add two stars.
3. Select the first star and click "Flip" and then select "Flip Vertical".
4. Align both stars to overlap them at the center.
5. Select "Weld" to make a new shape and add a scoreline.
6. Align them at the center and attach them.
7. Select the "Make it" button and then "Continue" to cut your card out.

If you don't know how to add text or write on a card, follow the processes below.

1. Select your choice of shape. Let's choose a hexagon for example. Select the "Shape" option and click on the hexagon shape.

2. Use your favorite pattern.
3. Add a scoring line and rotate it.
4. Click "Add Text". A box will appear on the canvas or work area of your project. Write your desired text. Let's say you choose to write "A Star Is Born Strong" and "And Rugged" on the two hexagonal shapes. Choose the fonts and style of writing.
5. Select the first text and flip vertically or horizontally.
6. Select the second text and flip vertically. Click, "Flip" and select flip vertically. Doing this will make the text not look upside down.
7. Select the "Make it" button and then "Continue" to cut your card out. Follow the cutting process on the screen to full effect.

How to Make a Simple T-Shirt?

You can use your Cricut Explore Air 2 to make nice T-shirt designs and it's quite easy to do. Cricut cuts out an iron-on vinyl design in an easy and simple way. I will teach you how to make a simple t-shirt with the Cricut Explore Air 2.

In this tutorial, we will be using iron-on vinyl. Iron-on vinyl is a type of vinyl, like an adhesive that will stick to any fabric when applied using an iron.

1. Log into your Design Space.

2. Select "New Project" and then, click on "Templates" in the top left corner. Choosing a template makes it easier to visualize your design to know how good or bad it will be on your T-shirt.
3. Choose "Classic T-Shirt" and pick your preferred style, size, and color.
4. You will see tons of beautiful designs for iron-on T-shirts. Browse through the images before you make your choice.
5. Remember, if your preferred design isn't available, you can upload your pictures to the Cricut Design Space. We have created a tutorial on how to upload your own images to Cricut Design Space.
6. After you have selected the image, resize the image to fit the T-shirt. You can do this by clicking the resize handle in the bottom part of your design and dragging the mouse to enlarge or reduce.
7. When you are done, click the "Make it" button in the top right corner. You will be told to connect your Cricut machine.
8. Toggle the green "Mirror" button on. Toggling it on will make sure your design is not cut backward.
9. Face the shiny part of your vinyl design down on your cutting mat. Remember to move the smart set dial to the iron-on option.
10. Remove all the vinyl designs you don't want to be transferred to your project when it's ironed. Use your

weeding tool to remove those little bits that will jeopardize your beautiful design. This process is called weeding.
11. Transfer your design to your T-shirt when you are done weeding. You can either use an iron or an EasyPress. Preheat your EasyPress before use.

How to Make a Leather Bracelet

The Cricut Explore Air 2 can be pretty amazing in doing a variety of things. One of those things is being able to make a leather bracelet with your Cricut. You can make pretty cool designs that you can turn into wearable pieces of jewelry.

To make a leather bracelet, you need your Cricut Explore Air 2, a deep point blade, faux leather, marker, ruler, craft knife, bracelet cut file, transfer tape, and a grip mat. You will also need glue, an EasyPress or iron and an SVG design to crown it up.

Follow these steps to create your leather bracelets.

1. Log into your Design Space account menu.
2. Select "Canvas".
3. Upload an art set from Jen Goode into the Design Space. The Jen Goode is a set of designs with 4 different image layouts.
4. Ungroup the designs and hide the layers you don't require after selecting your design.

5. Create a base cut of the shape you want to use. Use a cut file and create the shape you want. For example, you can use a shape tool to create a circular design.
6. Add circle cutouts with basic shapes. Duplicate the layer so that you will use it for the back of the bracelet.
7. Set your iron or EasyPress ready and apply the vinyl to the uppermost layer of your leather.
8. Spread a thin coat of glue on the back of the duplicated layer and press it with the other layer together.
9. Add your bracelet strap or chain together with some other ornaments.
10. Congratulations! You have just made your first leather bracelet.

Making a Stencil for Painting with the Cricut Explore Air 2

To make a stencil, you can either use the ready-made designs or make your own design. This tutorial will be based on how to create a stencil for painting.

1. Log in to your Design Space.
2. Click "Canvas" from the drop-down menu.
3. Click "Add Text".
4. Highlight text and change to your preferred font.
5. All your letters must be separated. If they aren't, click the ungroup button to separate. The letters must overlap. This will allow you to drag each letter as you please.

6. Arrange your text line as you want it. If you notice each letter is still showing individually, highlight the text box and click "Weld" at the bottom right of the panel.
7. Click "Attach". Make sure the text is highlighted. This will make the letters arranged properly when it goes to the cut mat.
8. Your stencil design is ready!

Making a Vinyl Sticker

First of all, you need to have an idea of the vinyl sticker that you want. Get ideas online or from forums. Once you have gotten the picture, make a sketch of it to see how the sticker would look. After you have done this, follow the steps below;

1. Use an image editing software like Photoshop or Illustrator. Design to your taste and save. Make sure you know the folder it is saved too.
2. Now, open your Design Space.
3. Click "New Project".
4. Scroll to the bottom left-hand side and click "Upload".
5. Drag and drop the design you created with your photo editing app.
6. Select your image type. If you want to keep your design simple, select simple.
7. Select which area of the image is not part of it.

8. Before you forge ahead, select the image as cut to have a preview. You can go back if there is a need for adjustments.
9. Select "Cut".
10. Weed excess vinyl.
11. Use a transfer tape on top of the vinyl. This will make the vinyl stay in position.
12. Go over the tape and ensure all the bibles are nowhere to be found.
13. Peel away the transfer tape and you have your vinyl sticker.

Chapter 11: Tips And Tricks To Make Cricut Machines Easier And Efficient

There are a lot of things which you can achieve by making the correct use of your machine. However, it is not just enough to know these; you need to know easier and more improved ways to make use of the machine you have acquired. To make the most out of your newly-acquired machine, here are a few things you should do.

Test Out Your Machine First

This is a no-brainer, and you should do it as soon as the machine arrives. It is always a safe idea to start by testing out the components of your machine and double-checking to ensure that your machine has all the accessories that were promised. If at this stage, you discover that your machine is missing a few things, you may want to reach out to membership support immediately and get the issues rectified.

Keep the Components of Your Machine (Especially the Cutting Mat) Clean

This is one of the parts of the machine that is constantly subjected to wear, tear, attack by dirt, and spoiling. In order to make sure that your machine remains in the best of conditions, take out time to clean your mat frequently. Best practices when you are trying to get this done is to make use of a lint roller to wipe down the mat after every use and to also scan over the mat once you are done with it to make sure that you take out all the little pieces that may remain from the materials you just cut. Also, be sure to frequently replace the plastic protective sheet that came with the mat, and it is not entirely unheard of for you to wash the mat frequently too. However, washing the mat can be a tricky business. Considering the fact that the mat is meant to be in a specific way, you need to make sure that you wash it in such a way that you do not compromise the integrity of the material the mat is made of. For best practices, wash with lukewarm water and mild dish soap. With these, scrub gently in circular patterns, rinse and allow the mat to drip dry.

Cutting Certain Materials Require for Your Mat to Be A Bit Sticky

So that it can hold the material you are looking to cut in place. Due to some factors like prolonged use, and continuous subjection to heavy work, there may be times that you would need to cut something that requires that the mat has a firm grip on the material, but you may not have access to a good mat that has not lost its stickiness at that time. As a way around this, you can resort to using masking tape or painter's tape to hold the material you are looking to cut in place. However, take this as a cue to change mats because this option won't work forever.

Pattern on Storing Blades

In order to prevent the confusion that can come as a result of having to deal with many blades that you will need for your different projects, it can be safe to adopt the pattern of storing up your blades in such a way that you can tell almost instantly what blade is used to cut what material. In essence, it is vital for you to learn to separate your blades. Let there be blades that you use to cut vinyl, then the ones you use to cut paper, and wood, and all the rest of them. This will ensure that your blades last for much longer and that you don't use the wrong blades for the wrong projects, thereby creating trouble for your new machine. You can get started by finding small jars to hold the blades, and then labeling each jar to signify which blades go into it. This way, you do not run the risk of making a mistake with your blade placement.

Color of Vinyl

You do not always have to have the right color of vinyl for you to embark upon your projects. Let's assume that you are about to get started with a project and you need some green vinyl, but all you have is pink-colored vinyl, you must not get dressed and go off to the mall to get the green-colored ones because there is a way around it. Instead of running off to the mall every time you need a different color of vinyl, why not get some Rust-Oleum Metallic Spray paint for the future. With this, you can give your un-cut vinyl some spraying and color-over without having to spend money every time. Just for a few bucks, you can get this over with.

Recommendable Websites

Dafont and **1001freefonts** are amazing websites where you can find tons of fonts that you can make use of to create even more epic designs. If you have searched through the design space and you have not been able to see something that piques your interests, or you just need to try out something new, you may want to visit those platforms and see what they have in store for you. Also, you will find a lot of support groups on Facebook where you can find a lot of helpful information in regards to your creative journey with the machine you have just acquired. Join these groups, and be sure to be an active member of them. You will see that there are some things that may bother you that can be a walkover for another person; all you need to do is reach out. Furthermore, these platforms serve as hosting sites for a ton of helpful tools that can even unclog your creativity even more. Find them as pinned documents, helpful DIY tips, post and comment threads, and in all other formats as they come. The goal is to make sure that you do not try to do this on your own.

Stenciling Tips

Want to do some stenciling, but you are not sure where and how you can get started?

There's no need for you to be confused when you can make use of freezer paper to create custom stencils for your projects. With the Cricut Explore Air 2, you can get to cut the paper and fashion it into some custom-design stencils for your projects.

Make Use of Tin Foils to Sharpen Your Blades.

Notwithstanding how careful you are with the blades, and how you do not mistake them for cutting different materials, it is not possible for your blades not to get to a point where they become blunt and weak. When your blades get blunt, a great way to get them up and running once again is by making use of tin foils to sharpen them. By sharpening with tin foil, you can extend the life of your blade, almost by x3. Sharpening is very simple, all you need to do is to unclamp the blade and run the tip of the blade through the tin foil between 10-15 times.

Using Pens Other Than the Cricut Pens to Write

Next to the Cricut pens, there are a ton of other brands that you can make use of, even with your machine. They include:

- Uni-ball Signo UM-153.
- Tombow Dual brush pens.
- Sakura gelly roll.

- Bic marking and Bic crystal.
- Pilot Precise.

The list is basically endless. The best part is that for all these pens, you can find them online, and with just a few dollars, you can have them added to your bucket list of pens to work with. However, to make use of these pens with your machine, you need a pen adapter. Pen adapters work for the Explore Air 2 or newer models of the Cricut machine. With these, you can connect any brand of Cricut pens and draw/write away.

Increase Your Image Options by Learning How to Make Your Own SVG Files Online.

While the design space and the internet provide you with endless numbers of images, you will agree that there are those times when even the most intricately designed picture does not quite cut it; it does not do justice to what you want to create. Under these circumstances, you need to learn how to bring your inner genius to life.

Using Inkscape, you can create your own SVG files from scratch or convert your boring pictures to two-layered SVG files. Inkscape is a free tool that you can make use of, and making use of it is relatively easy.

Chapter 12: Best Software To Use With Cricut And Create Super Design Templates

Design Space

Design Space is for any Explore machine with a high-speed, broadband Internet connection that is connected to a computer or an iOS device. This more advanced software allows full creative control for users with Cricut machines.

Craft Room

Some machines, such as the Explore and Explore Air, cannot use Craft Room, but many other models can. Craft Room users also have access to a free digital cartridge, which offers images that all Cricut machines can cut.

Moving on to Creating Your Project Template

On the home page, select "New Project", which will be followed by a page with a blank canvas that looks like the grid on your Cricut mats. To any artist, the words "empty canvas" is a nightmare in themselves so please just bear with me since we will fill that bad boy up in a second. But first, let's go through the menu options.

New, Templates, Projects, Images, Text, Shapes, and Upload; these are the things that you will see on your left-hand side when you have the canvas open on the screen.

- New

New means that you will start a new project and clicking the tab will redirect you to a blank canvas. Be sure to save all changes on your current project before you go to the new canvas. Otherwise, you will lose all of the progress you have already made on that design.

- Templates

Clicking on Templates will allow you to set a template to help you visualize and work with sizing. It is very handy for someone who is not familiar with Cricut Design Space and doesn't know what sizes to set. If you are cutting out wearable items on fabric, you can change the size of the template to fit whoever will be wearing it. I'm sure you can agree that this feature is especially beneficial for the seamstresses out there.

- Projects

Projects, meanwhile, will lead you to the ready-to-make projects so that you can start cutting right away. Some of the projects are not customizable, but others are when you open the template, which is pretty cool. Many of these are not free either, which irks me to a new extent. You can choose the "Free for Cricut (whatever machine you have)", and the projects that will turn up won't have to be paid for.

- Images

Images are where you can search for thousands of photos to use for the craft. Those images with the green flag with the "A" on them are the ones that come only with Cricut Access so be aware if you do not have it. It is sort of like a Pinterest image search engine with a lot of pictures in its database.

- Text

The Text basically goes without saying. When you select this option, you can type whatever you want and scale it onto your canvas. You may select any font saved in your computer too; that's why collecting those has never been more useful! There is also an option called "multi-layered font", which gives your text a shadow layer. If you are cutting out the letters and shadow layers, the Cricut will do them separately and combine the two later if you wish to. It can create very cool effects so make sure you try that option out. Furthermore, remember that when you are being paid to do a job, the font you are using might require a license to use.

- Shapes

Shapes lets you add basic forms to your canvas, which you can tweak to fit your own needs. The shapes include circle, square, rectangle, triangle, etc.

- Upload

When you click the Upload tab, you can upload your own images and transform them into cuttable pieces. This, along with the text, is the only reason why I still use Design Space. It is really awesome to be able to use this feature.

Cricut Basic

This is a program or software designed to help the new user get an easy start on designing new crafts and DIY projects. This system will help you with the image-selection for cutting in the least amount of time spent on the design stages. You can locate your image, pre-set projector font, and immediately print, cut, score, and align with tools that are found within the program. You can use this program on the iOS 7.1.2 or later systems as well as iPad and several of the iPhones, from the Mini to the 5th generation iPod touch. Since it is also a cloud-based service, you are able to start on one device and finish from another.

Sure, Cuts a Lot

This is another third-party software that has a funny name that gives you the ability to take control of your designs without some of the limitations that can happen when using cartridges used within the Cricut Design Studio. You will need to install an update to your software to use this program; you can download it for free. It allows for the use of TrueType and OpenType font formats as well as simple drawing and editing tools. You can import any file format and then convert it to the one that you need. There is an option for blackout and shadow.

Cricut Design Studio

This program allows you to connect with your software and provides you with much more functionality as far as shapes and fonts are concerned. There are various options for tools that provide you resources for designing more creative images. You will be able to flip, rotate, weld, or slant the images and fonts. However, you will still be limited in the amounts or types of fonts that you can use based on the ones on the cartridges. There is a higher level of software features that allow for customization.

Cricut Sync

This is a program designed for updating the Cricut Expression 2 as well as the Imagine machine and the Gypsy device. You just connect your system to the computer and run the synced program for an installation of updates on the features that come with your machine. This is also used to troubleshoot any issues that could arise from the hardware.

Play Around and Practice

You can combine your shapes and images, add some text, and create patterns. The possibilities are endless. The best thing to do is familiarize yourself with the software before you attempt on cutting expensive materials. Start small and cheap - printer paper will be an ideal choice - and cut away. See what works well for you and stick with it. There are many options concerning the Cricut Design Space, and the only way to learn all of this is to experiment and click on every tab you see and try different combinations and options when playing around on the software.

Make the Cut

This is a third-party program that works with the Cricut design software. It offers a straightforward look at the design features that Cricut has. This system can convert a raster image into a vector so that you can cut it. There is also a great way to do lattice tools. It uses many file formats and TrueType fonts. There are advanced tools for editing and an interface that is easy to learn and use. This system works with Craft ROBO, Gazelle, Silhouette, Wishblade, and others. It allows you to import any file from a TTF, OTF, PDF, GSD, and so on and convert them to JPG, SVG, PDF, and so on. It is flexible and user-friendly.

Conclusion

If you are a craft blogger, then this machine was built for people like you in mind. Purchasing the Cricut depends entirely on your needs and how often you make crafts. If you love to craft, make personalized projects, you do plenty of scrapbooking—then this machine will save time and money for you in the long run.

How often you use the Cricut will also determine whether this machine is worth the price. Would you use it once every three months? Would you only use it when Christmas is around the corner, and you want to make personalized gifts? Would you use it every week? Do you want to make labels and stickers for your business? Do you want to have a machine that helps you create signage for your events or catering business?

All the answers to these questions will determine if the Cricut is indeed worth its money. One of the ways to use the machine as many times as possible is to consider turning your crafting hobby into a side income.

Focusing on online-selling requires a higher technical knowledge base; yet, as I can confirm, you don't need to be a programmer to make it work. You can generate income with vinyl online by offering top-quality personalized jobs, ending up being a details

Centre, or supplying bulk offerings. Again, it's not advisable to try to do it all.

Your time is ideal invested working in among these three alternatives to begin. So, if you decide to give a custom job, don't additionally attempt to become an info hub at the same time. After developing your initial footing, and obtaining profitable sales, you can intend on how to use that cash to turn into the other classifications.

Personalized Job-- This is just how I obtained my beginning. For the best individual, I truly believe this is a fantastic means to kick off your Silhouette or Cricut vinyl business.

Progressively, individuals are resorting to a Google search to find a custom-made job. With existing markets or your website, you can end up being the one they rely on.

Examples:

Existing web sites that permit you to offer custom-made design solutions.

- Etsy
- Amazon Personalized
- Amazon Handmade is the most widely known.

Various other options consist of:

- Artfire
- DaWanda

- Gold Mine
- Depop
- Tictail.

One more option is to release your very own website. A fantastic instance of this can be seen with "A Wonderful Impression". They released an inspirational wall decal website, along with a custom-made layout solution. You can get any kind of sticker, in any type of dimension you desire from them.

If you sell on an existing system, the startup costs are more reduced. The minute you launch, you're competing in the worldwide marketplace. You have access to countless prospective clients.

Additionally, distinct designs will certainly permit you to bill a premium price. However, on the internet, custom costs tend to be lower than the very same work done locally. It's a chance to polish up and increase your design capability as well.

www.ingramcontent.com/pod-product-compliance
Lightning Source LLC
Chambersburg PA
CBHW071529080526
44588CB00011B/1603